I Won't Learn from You!

assent: The act of the mind
   in accepting as true or
   certain something proposed
   for belief, as a doctrine or
   conclusion. mental consent

I Won't Learn from You!

THE ROLE OF ASSENT
IN LEARNING

Herbert Kohl

Milkweed Editions
Thistle Series

I WON'T LEARN FROM YOU!
The Role of Assent in Learning

© 1991, Text by Herbert Kohl
© 1991, Design by R. W. Scholes
All rights reserved.
Printed in the United States of America
Published in 1991 by *Milkweed Editions*
Post Office Box 3226
Minneapolis, Minnesota 55403
Books may be ordered at the above address

ISBN 0-915943-64-6

Publication of this book is made possible by grant support from the
Literature Program of the National Endowment for the Arts, the Cowles
Media/Star Tribune Foundation, the Dayton Hudson Foundation for
Daytons and Target Stores, the First Bank System Foundation, the General
Mills Foundation, the I. A. O'Shaughnessy Foundation, the Jerome Founda-
tion, the Minnesota State Arts Board through an appropriation by the
Minnesota Legislature, the Northwest Area Foundation, and by the support of
generous individuals.

Library of Congress Cataloging-in-Publication Data

Kohl, Herbert R.
    I won't learn from you / Herbert Kohl.
        p.   cm.
    ISBN 0-915943-64-6   ∞
    1. Learning.   I. Title.
LB1060.K65   1991
370.15'23 — dc20   90-25969
                        CIP

*Dedicated to the memory of Betty Rawls
and the continuing struggle for justice*

I Won't Learn from You!

Years ago, one of my fifth-grade students told me that his grandfather Wilfredo wouldn't learn to speak English. He said that no matter how hard you tried to teach him, Wilfredo ignored whatever words you tried to teach and forced you to speak to him in Spanish. When I got to know his grandfather I asked, in Spanish, whether I could teach him English, and he told me unambiguously that he did not want to learn. He was frightened, he said, that his grandchildren would never learn Spanish if he gave in like the rest of the adults and spoke English with the children. Then, he said, they would not know who they were. At the end of our conversation he repeated adamantly that nothing could make him learn to speak English, that families and cultures could not survive if the children lost their parents' language and finally that learning what others wanted you to learn can sometimes destroy you.

When I discussed Wilfredo's reflections with several friends, they interpreted his remarks as a cover-up of either his fear of trying to learn English or his failure to do so. These explanations, however, show a lack of respect for Wilfredo's ability to judge what is appropriate learning for himself and for his grandchildren. By attributing failure to Wilfredo and by refusing to acknowledge the loss his family would experience through not knowing Spanish, they turned a cultural problem into a personal psychological problem: they turned willed refusal to learn into failure to learn.

I've thought a lot about Wilfredo's conscious refusal to learn English and have great sympathy for his decision. I grew up in a partially bilingual family, in a house shared by my parents, born in New York City, and my grandparents, born in the Yiddish-speaking Polish part of the Jewish settlements in Eastern Europe called the Pale. I know what it is like to face the problem of not-learning and the dissolution of culture. In addition, I have encountered willed not-learning throughout my thirty years of teaching and believe that such not-learning is often and disastrously mistaken for failure to learn or the inability to learn.

Learning how to not-learn is an intellectual and social challenge; sometimes you have to work very hard at it. It consists of an active, often ingenious, willful rejection of even the most compassionate and well-designed teaching. It subverts attempts at remediation as much as it rejects learning in the first place. It was through insight into my own not-learning that I began to understand the inner world of students who chose to not-learn what I wanted to teach. Over the years I've come to side with them in their refusal to be molded by a hostile society and have come to look upon not-learning as positive and healthy in many situations.

Before looking in detail at some of my students' not-learning and the intricate ways in which it was part of their self-respect and identity, I want to share one of my own early ventures into not-learning and self-definition. I cannot speak Yiddish, though I have had opportunities to learn from the time I was born. My father's parents spoke Yiddish most of the time and since my family lived downstairs from them in a two-family house for fourteen of my first seventeen years, my failure to learn wasn't from lack of exposure. My father speaks both Yiddish and English and never indicated that he wouldn't teach me Yiddish. Nor did he ever try to coerce me to learn the language, so I never had educational traumas associated with learning Yiddish. My mother and her family had everything to do with it. They didn't speak Yiddish at all. Learning Yiddish meant being party to conversations that excluded my mother. I didn't reject my grandparents and their language. It's just that I didn't want to be included in conversations unless my mother was also included. In solidarity with her, I learned how to not-learn Yiddish.

There was Yiddish to be heard everywhere in my environment, except at public school: on the streets, at home, in every store. Learning to not-learn Yiddish meant that I had to forget Yiddish words as soon as I heard them. When words stuck in my head I had to refuse to associate the sounds with any meaning. If someone told a story in Yiddish, I had to talk to myself quietly in English or hum to myself. If a relative greeted me in Yiddish I responded with the uncomprehending look I had rehearsed for those occasions. I also remember learning to concentrate on the component sounds of words and thus shut out the speaker's meaning or intent. In doing so, I allowed myself to be satisfied with understanding the emotional flow of a conversation without knowing what people were saying. I was doing just the reverse of what beginning readers are expected to do—read words and understand meanings instead of getting stuck on particular letters and the sounds they make. In effect I used phonics to obliterate meaning.

In not-learning Yiddish, I had to ignore phrases and gestures, even whole conversations, as well as words. And there were many lively, interesting conversations upstairs at my grandparents'. They had meetings about union activities, talked about family matters and events in Europe and later in Israel. They discussed articles in the *Daily Forward*, the Yiddish newspaper, and plays downtown in the Yiddish theater. Everyone was a poet, and everybody had an opinion. I let myself read hands and faces, and I imagined ideas and opinions bouncing around the room. I experienced these conversations much in the way I learned to experience Italian opera when I was fourteen. I had a sense of plot and character and could follow the flow and drama of personal interaction, yet I had no idea of the specifics of what was being said. To use another image: it was as if I were at a foreign-language movie with my father, my uncles, and my grandmother providing English subtitles whenever I asked for help understanding what was going on. I allowed myself to be content with this partial knowledge, but now I mourn the loss of the language and culture of my father's family that it entailed.

Deciding to actively not-learn something involves closing off part of oneself and limiting one's experience. It can require actively refusing to pay attention, acting dumb, scrambling one's thoughts, and overriding curiosity. The balance of gains and losses resulting from such a turning away from experience is difficult to assess. I still can't tell how much I gained or lost by not-learning Yiddish. I know that I lost a language that would have enriched my life, but I gained an understanding of the psychology of active not-learning that has been very useful to me as a teacher.

Because not-learning involves willing rejection of some aspect of experience, it can often lead to what appears to be failure. For example, in the case of some youngsters, not-learning to read can be confused with failing to learn to read if the rejection of learning is overlooked as a significant factor. I had that happen to me when I was eleven and expanded not-learning Yiddish to not-learning Hebrew. I was sent to *chedah*, Hebrew school, to learn that part of the Torah that I would have to read aloud in front of the whole congregation during my bar mitzvah. My family was not at all religious, and though we belonged to a temple, we attended services only on Yom Kippur. From my perspective, the point of going to Hebrew school was not to learn Hebrew but to ensure that I didn't embarrass my parents when I had to recite part of the Torah on my bar mitzvah. As I figured it, if I not-learned Hebrew it would save me a lot of effort and time I could use for science projects and my rather tentative experiments with writing. And so for two years I applied what I had learned about not-learning Yiddish and I not-learned Hebrew. I could read the sounds and recite my way through the *Mahzor*, the daily prayer book, and the Torah. I listened to our teacher/rabbi drone on about the righteousness of the Jews and our special role in history, and I was silent though cynical.

I did, however, get in trouble for my arrogant not-learning. One day the rabbi gave us a test with questions written in Hebrew. Since I couldn't translate a word from Hebrew to English, much less an entire question, my prospects for passing the test were not good. I was too proud to show the rabbi that I couldn't do the test, so I set it up with my friend Ronnie that I would copy his test. Cheating in Hebrew school was not a moral issue to me but a matter of saving face. Ronnie understood my dilemma perfectly and told me he would have loved to not-learn Hebrew too, only his father insisted on testing him every night on his Hebrew school lessons.

During the test I succeeded in copying Ronnie's whole paper which I knew was a sure "A," only I failed worse than if I had written letters at random in mock Hebrew on the test sheet. The rabbi returned all of the papers except Ronnie's and mine. Then he called the class to attention and said he felt a need to give special appreciation to Ronnie, for not only had Ronnie gotten one "A," he also received a second "A" which, the rabbi said, was the first time in his career that any student had done that well. And, he added, Herbert didn't hand in any paper at all, which he told the class was worse than trying and failing. It seems that I had copied Ronnie's paper so accurately that I had answered the Hebrew question "What is your name?" with Ronnie's Hebrew name. I was thoroughly humiliated in front of all of my friends and, for all my arrogance about getting away with not-learning Hebrew, felt very stupid.

I never forgot this humiliation, and when I became a teacher I resolved never to humiliate any of my students. I also decided to assume that there were complex factors behind any apparent failure which, if understood, could be used to transform it into positive learning. Not-learning Yiddish and Hebrew has made me very sensitive to the difference between not-learning and failing to learn. Failure is characterized by the frustrated will to know, whereas not-learning involves the will to refuse knowledge. Failure results from a mismatch between what the learner wants to do and is able to do. The reasons for failure may be personal, social, or cultural, but whatever they are, the results of failure are most often a loss of self-confidence accompanied by a sense of inferiority and inadequacy. Not-learning produces thoroughly different effects. It tends to strengthen the will, clarify one's definition of self, reinforce self-discipline, and provide inner satisfaction. Not-learning can also get one in trouble if it results in defiance or a refusal to become socialized in ways that are sanctioned by dominant authority.

Not-learning tends to take place when someone has to deal with unavoidable challenges to her or his personal and

15

family loyalties, integrity, and identity. In such situations there are forced choices and no apparent middle ground. To agree to learn from a stranger who does not respect your integrity causes a major loss of self. The only alternative is to not-learn and reject the stranger's world.

In the course of my teaching career I have seen children choose to not-learn many different skills, ideas, attitudes, opinions, and values. At first I confused not-learning with failing. When I had youngsters in my classes who were substantially "behind" in reading, I assumed that they had failed to learn how to read. Therefore I looked for the sources of their failure in the reading programs they were exposed to, in their relationships with teachers and other adults in authority, and in the social and economic conditions of their lives. I assumed that something went wrong when they faced a written text, that either they made errors they didn't know how to correct or they were the victims of bad teaching.

Other causes of failure I searched for were mismatches between the students' language and the language of the schools or between the students' experiences and the kind of experience presupposed by their teachers or the reading texts. In all of these cases I assumed that my students had failed at something they had tried to do. Sometimes I was correct, and then it was easy to figure out a strategy to help them avoid old errors and learn, free of failure. But there were many cases I came upon where obviously intelligent students were beyond success or failure when it came to reading or other school-related learning. They had consciously placed themselves outside the entire system that was trying to coerce or seduce them into learning and spent all their time and energy in the classroom devising ways of not-learning, short-circuiting the business of failure altogether. They were engaged in a struggle of wills with authority, and what seemed to be at stake for them was nothing less than their pride and integrity. Most of them did not believe that they were failures or that they were inferior to students who succeeded on the schools' terms, and they were easy to distinguish from the wounded self-effacing students who wanted to learn but had not been able to do so.

I remember one student, Barry, who was in one of my combined kindergarten/first-grade classes in Berkeley in the 1970s. He had been held back in the first grade by his previous teacher for being uncooperative, defiant, and "not ready for the demands of second grade." He was sent to my class because it was multi-age graded, and the principal hoped I could get him to catch up and go on with other students his age by the end of the year. Barry was confident and cocky but not rude. From his comments in class it was clear that he was quite sensitive and intelligent. The other students in the class respected him as the best fighter and athlete in class, and as a skilled and funny storyteller.

During the first week of school, one of the students mentioned to me that their last year's teacher had been afraid of Barry. I've seen a number of cases where white teachers treat very young African American boys as if they were seventeen, over six feet tall, addicted to drugs and menacing. Barry was a victim of that manifestation of racism. He had evidently been given the run of the school the previous year—had been allowed to wander the halls at will, refuse participation in group activities, and avoid any semblance of academic work. Consequently he fell behind and was not promoted from first to second grade.

The first time I asked Barry to sit down and read with me he threw a temper tantrum and called me all kinds of names. We never got near a book. I had to relate to his behavior, not his reading. There was no way for me to discover the level of his skills or his knowledge of how reading works. I tried to get him to read a few more times and watched his responses to me very carefully. His tantrums clearly were manufactured on the spot. They were a strategy of not-reading. He never got close enough to a book to have failed to learn how to read.

The year before, this response had the effect he wanted. He was let alone and, as a bonus, gained status in the eyes of the other children as being someone teachers feared. Not-reading, as tragic as it might become in his future, was very successful for him as a kindergartner. My job as a teacher was to get him to feel more empowered by reading than by practicing his active not-learning to read.

I developed a strategy of empowerment for Barry and didn't even bother to think about remediation. I was convinced he could learn to read perfectly well if he assented to learn how to read. The strategy was simple and involved a calculated risk. I decided to force him to read with me and then make it appear to other members of the class that he could read well, and that his past resistance was just a game he controlled. The goal was to have him show me up in class, as if his past failure was a joke he was playing on us all, and have him display to the entire class a reading ability he didn't know he had.

I prepared myself for a bit of drama. One Monday afternoon I asked Barry to come read with me. Naturally, all the other students stopped what they were doing and waited for the show. They wanted to see if Barry would be able to not-read one more time. He looked at me, then turned around and walked away. I picked up a book, went over to him, gently but firmly sat him down in a chair, and sat down myself. Before he could throw the inevitable tantrum I opened the book and said, "Here's the page you have to read. It says, 'This is a bug. This is a jug. This is a bug in the jug.' Now read it to me." He started to squirm and put his hands over his eyes. Only I could see a sly grin forming as he sneaked a look at the book. I had given him the answers, told him exactly what he had to do to show me and the rest of the class that he knew how to read all along. It was his decision: to go on playing his not-learning game or accept my face-saving gift and open up the possibility of learning to read. I offered him the possibility of entering into a teaching/learning relationship with me without forcing him to give up any of his status, and fortunately he accepted the gift. He mumbled, "This is a bug, this is a jug, this is a bug in a jug," then tossed the book on the floor, and, turning to one of the other children, said defiantly, "See, I told you I already know how to read."

This ritual battle was repeated all week and into the next, subsiding slowly as he felt that the game was no longer necessary and that he was figuring out the relationship of letters to sounds, words, and meanings. After a while, reading became just another one of the things that Barry did in class. I never did any remedial teaching or treated him as a failed reader. In fact, I was able to reach him by acknowledging his choice to not-learn and by tricking him out of it. However, if he had refused assent, there is no way I could have forced him to learn to read. That was a very important lesson to me. It helped me understand the essential role that will and free choice play in learning, and it taught me the importance of considering people's stance towards learning in the larger context of the choices they make as they create lives and identities for themselves.

Over the years I've known many youngsters who chose to actively not-learn what their school, society, or family tried to teach them. Not all of them were potential victims of their own choices to not-learn. For some not-learning was a strategy that made it possible for them to function on the margins of society instead of falling into madness or total despair. It helped them build a small, safe world in which their feelings of being rejected by family and society could be softened. Not-learning played a positive role and enabled them to take control of their lives and get through difficult times. Recently I encountered a young man I've known since he was in elementary school who has become a master of not-learning and has turned it into an artistic life form. Rick, who is nineteen, has consciously chosen to reject the conventional values of middle-class life. Through his poetry, he scorns and criticizes such pious values as hard work, obedience, patriotism, loyalty, and money. He honed his not-learning skills in elementary school and became particularly adept at them in junior high school. An articulate, conscious not-learner, Rick is very explicit about his achievements. He claims that the most difficult not-learning he ever did was in introductory algebra, which he failed three times. Rick is very quick in math, and there were no intellectual reasons he couldn't learn algebra.

There were emotional reasons Rick refused to learn algebra, but it's essential to distinguish here between his decision to not-learn algebra and his ability to learn it. Rick could have learned algebra quite easily. There was nothing wrong with his mind, his ability to concentrate, or his ability to deal with abstract ideas. He could read, and he did read books he chose. He knew how to do very complex building projects and science experiments. He enjoyed playing around with athletic statistics and gambling odds. He just rejected the whole idea of being tested and measured against other students and, though he was forced to attend school, there was no way to force him to perform. He refused to learn and through that refusal gained power over his parents and teachers. As a free autonomous individual he chose to not-learn, and that was what his parents and the school authorities didn't know how to deal with.

It's interesting how stuck parents and school authorities are on a single way to live and learn. Any youngster who refuses to perform as demanded is treated as a major threat to the entire system. Experts are consulted, complex personal or family causes are fabricated, special programs are invented, all to protect the system from changing itself and accommodating difference. People like Rick then get channeled into marginal school experiences and, too often, marginalized lives.

Rick told me that not-learning algebra was an intriguing challenge, since he felt that the abstract representation of complex mathematical relationships might interest him as much as chess did. In order to force failure, Rick found ingenious ways to dissolve equations into marks on the page by creating visual exercises that treated the equations as non-mathematical markings. For example, one exercise consisted of reading an equation from the equal sign out in a number of steps so that he would read $3a+2b=12a-32$ as the sequence: $=$, $b=1$, $2b=12$, $+2b=12a$, $a+2b=12a-$, etc. Sometimes he would even memorize the sequence.

When his teacher asked him what he was doing he explained exactly what his procedure was, infuriating the teacher more than if he had merely said he didn't understand the problem.

Rick's rejection of authority is sincere, well thought out, and based on a personal analysis of some unsettling experiences he has had in his family life. There is fear of the world and personal insecurity in his rejection, too. He believes that people should not judge each other, that they should live with minimal possessions and take pleasure from each other's company and from their own creative abilities. Rick, who is a musician, is an anarchist who lives his beliefs. He left school, moved out of his home, and now lives communally with other members of his band and a few other friends. Their ambition, in addition to making music and art, is to live free of institutional control and to restore some peace and sanity to an earth they see pulled apart by greed and competition.

Consistent with this philosophy, Rick told me that he has not-learned many things which go against his beliefs. Some of them appear extreme, but none of them harm anybody or hurt the earth though they do offend social customs. For example, he has not-learned to wear shoes and has developed a whole series of strategies so that he can manage to get into places where shoes are required or expected, such as restaurants or theaters. Rick distinguishes not-learning to wear shoes from simply refusing to wear shoes. The difference is manifested in Rick's total lack of hostility when people tell him that shoes are required or expected. Rick's response is that he's sorry about it but he can't wear shoes. In successfully not-learning to wear shoes despite the pressure on him to wear them, it's no longer an issue for him and therefore he has avoided the defiant attitude of someone who merely refuses to wear shoes.

More generally, Rick is not asking to be accepted or rejected for what he does. Being left alone to be as he pleases is enough. He has chosen how he will and won't be socialized, what he'll learn and what he'll not-learn. Many of his arguments against consumerism and the arrogant wastefulness of our society are convincing. In some ways his life is healthier and saner than the norm. Unfortunately there are people who represent the institutions of conformity of our society and resent Rick's choice to not conform. They try to categorize, stigmatize, and even institutionalize and punish him. He refuses to learn to act according to their definitions of him. He says he'll not-learn to be crazy or criminal and won't be driven to give up his autonomy and sanity by accepting their right to invalidate his experiences and stigmatize him. I don't know how Rick will make out in the future. I worry that the rejection he has experienced will finally wear him down and that he'll turn nasty or go crazy.

It may be that he'll also find that one day he'll wish he knew things he'd not-learned. That happened to me when, in September of 1954, I left the Bronx for Harvard, encountered my first Protestants, and found myself wishing I could speak Hebrew. In my neighborhood in the Bronx and at the Bronx High School of Science, I never considered myself a member of an ethnic or racial minority since I wasn't. Most of the people in my neighborhood and at school were Jewish. I wasn't naive—I knew that Jews were persecuted, that we were a sometimes rejected and despised ethnic minority in the United States. But on an everyday level I lived with Jews, went to school with Jews, and for the most part socialized with Jews. In my neighborhood, in addition to Jews there were Italians and Irish, and a smattering of African Americans and Puerto Ricans. In high school, my few non-Jewish friends were African American, Irish, or Italian. Before I went to Harvard I was accustomed to living in a daily world in which I was part of the majority, and I acted and lived without that caution, suspicion, and self-consciousness minorities often develop when they have daily contact with a dominant majority.

At Harvard, I soon realized that the social world was thoroughly different from the one I grew up in. Not only did white Protestant males dominate my freshmen dorm (Harvard was all male then) but I felt they enjoyed indulging that dominance by bringing up the issue of my Jewishness and of my working-class background. This may have been done in a spirit of goodwill, but I couldn't experience it that way. During all-night bull sessions I was asked about the Bronx, about Judaism, about the way my family lived, all in a way that seemed to preclude my asking them about their backgrounds. I was the curiosity, they were the norm. One student on my floor urged me to come with him to Memorial Chapel to hear Reinhold Niebuhr preach so that I could be exposed to the sophistication and relevance of contemporary Protestant thinking. Another urged me to read the New Testament, informing me that no educated person could live without knowing it. And then I remember conversations about people and places I had never heard of, prep school talk that made me feel very much a foreigner.

My problem was compounded by a number of other Jewish students who were also discovering their everyday minority status and were responding to it by becoming aggressively Jewish. They pressured me to join Hillel, the Jewish student organization, in order to alleviate some of the stress by spending time in a self-segregated Jewish environment where the illusion of being part of a majority could be reestablished.

I wanted to be myself, neither minority nor majority, and rejected both the pressure to assimilate and to separate. It was very hard to walk that thin line alone, yet there was no one to talk to about my desire to learn everything Harvard had to offer without giving up myself. And I thought a lot about my father's parents those days. They had come from Eastern Europe through Germany and England to the United States.

They didn't try to assimilate and didn't fall into any protective religious orthodoxy. My grandfather maintained his socialist vision of one big union of all peoples and cultures and must have thought about the problems I was now facing. If only I could speak to him intimately, personally, find out his ideas, learn his thoughts about his own experiences and hear his words, not as songs or through translations, but as meanings. I wished I spoke Yiddish and felt angry at myself for having willfully refused to learn it. Only when it was too late did I only understand what I had lost by not-learning Yiddish. The voice I needed to hear and to call on in my own musings about identity was not there for me. I managed to limp along and after a while discovered, first through reading, and later through traveling and finding friends, voices and people that helped me understand how to cross boundaries of class and culture without losing my own identity. However, I'm convinced that it has been a longer and more painful voyage than it might have been, had I known the language my grandparents spoke.

Akmir, a young African American man I had the privilege of knowing for the last three years of his life, was wiser than I was and struggled to learn and maintain his culture and learn his roots despite a racist school system that he was required to attend. In school he was a passionate not-learner. I remember him telling me of spending a semester in a junior high school social studies class not merely not-learning the subject but actively trying to destroy the teacher's and textbook's credibility. Akmir had joined a militant separatist group that was an offshoot of the Nation of Islam. They believed that they were among the 7% of African Americans who understood the truth that the white man was a devil and had to be ruthlessly rooted out and destroyed. One of their goals was purifying Harlem of all whites.

Akmir's experiences with whites did very little to refute the 7%ers' analysis. That opinion accurately applied to one of Akmir's high school history teachers who believed that his students, who were African American and Puerto Rican, were stupid, lazy, and incapable of understanding complex ideas. He talked to the class in a condescending manner, addressing them as "you" as in "You people don't know how to hold a job," and "You people have never learned to adopt American values and that's why you can't compete in the marketplace."

Most of the students were content to not-learn what he taught by playing dumb. A few actually learned what he taught and believed that they were stupid and incapable of productive lives. Akmir and one friend, Thomas X, were actively defiant. They not only refused to learn what he taught but tried to take over the class and change the curriculum into an attack on white racism. Whenever he talked about American values, for example, they would point out that slavery was an American value according to the Constitution and would try to demonstrate that racism, not lack of intelligence or ability, was the root of black failure and poverty. The teacher tried to shut them up, referred them to the guidance counselor, sent them to the principal, and in every way but answering their challenges, tried to silence them. Nothing worked, because Akmir and Thomas X refused to accept the validity of school authority and preached to the principal and the counselors the same line they preached in class. After one semester of bitter struggle at this school, both Akmir and Thomas X were transferred to a special school for discipline problems. These were schools for youngsters who had mastered strategies of not-learning and infuriated school authorities but had done nothing wrong. The schools were created to separate, within an already racially segregated system, teachers who were failing their students from their angry victims.

I didn't know Akmir until three years after he left high school. He had passed all of his classes, but his diploma had been withheld from him for "citizenship" reasons. The principal and guidance counselor decided that he wasn't a loyal American since he raised questions which they interpreted as anti-American. They decided that he didn't deserve to graduate because of this attitude and decreed that he had to take and pass a course in citizenship sometime during the two years after his class graduated in order to receive the diploma he had rightfully earned by passing all the required courses. They also told him that sometime in the future they would decide what work or school experience could count as a citizenship class. Akmir told them what he thought of them before leaving the school for what he believed was the last time.

At the time (it was 1965), I was a graduate student at Teachers College, Columbia University, and Betty Rawls, another graduate student, and I were teaching a class in psychology for a group of high-school-aged students who were older brothers and sisters of former students of mine from Harlem. Brenda

Jackson, one of the students, brought Akmir to class one day. They were a bit late, and when they arrived the class was discussing whether Freudian ideas applied to teenagers growing up in Harlem. The discussion was quite lively, but when Brenda and Akmir came into the room everyone fell silent. Brenda sat down, but Akmir remained standing and looked straight at me. I noticed how strong he looked, both physically and mentally.

Since everyone else in the room remained silent, I talked about my understanding of Freud and brought up some questions I had about some main Freudian concepts. After about five minutes Akmir took a few steps towards the front of the room and said quietly but fiercely, "That's white man's psychology."

I didn't disagree and suggested he go into his reasons for making that statement. He said there was no point in doing it for a white man, whereupon I told him he was wrong, adding that though Freud was a white man, he was also a bourgeois Viennese Jew who had grown up in the late 1800s and that it was unclear whether his ideas were adequate to account for the psychology of non-Jews, of working-class people, of women, and of young people in the 1960s, as well as of blacks.

He pushed aside my comments and began a harangue on racism, injustice, and the Wilderness of North America, which was the way Black Muslims referred to the United States. I grew angry and told him that the class was voluntary, that he could leave if he wanted to, but that we were there to learn together, and I wasn't bullshitting about wanting to know his ideas. Any intelligent position could be presented, defended, and argued, but learning couldn't take place without respect for everybody's voice.

The students glanced anxiously back and forth from Akmir to me. I rested my case and he smiled and said, "Well, maybe we should start with ego psychology and see what ego means for white people and for black people." I agreed, and we entered into that discussion.

After class Akmir came up and introduced himself. I told him that his questions and challenges were just what the class needed and invited him to join us. Betty and I usually assigned material to be read for each class, but since most of the students didn't get around to reading it, we began each class summarizing the issues we intended to discuss. Akmir read everything, studied it thoroughly, and came to class prepared to argue. He read all of the material aggressively, looking for sentences or phrases that indicated or could be interpreted to imply racism, ranging from uses of the words "black" or "dark" to signify evil to sophisticated arguments that implied the superiority of Western culture. For a few sessions the class was dominated by his questioning of our texts. At first I thought it was a game meant to provoke me, but it soon became clear that that was an egotistic response on my part. Akmir was hunting down American English for insinuations of racism and was trying to purify the language. He had learned some of these techniques from the Black Muslims and 7%ers, who were very skillful in hunting out claims of European pureness and African primitivity and who understood that when sophisticated Westerners were contrasted with un-sophisticated peoples of color, racism was afoot. I learned from Akmir's analyses how I too fell into sloppy, racist lin-guistic habits and came to take his criticisms seriously. I tried to read texts from his point of view and pick out the phrases and thoughts that he might find offensive. In some cases, it made reading familiar material very uncomfortable. I had thought of having the class analyze Conrad's *Heart of Dark-ness* from a psychoanalytic point of view but decided to abandon that exercise because, on rereading it with Akmir's sensitivities in mind, the explicit and offensive racism at the heart of the story appalled me. I had known before that the story could be interpreted as racist, but had always felt that that was just a secondary, unfortunate aspect of an ex-traordinary piece of writing. This time, though the quality of the writing wasn't diminished by my new reading, the story became repugnant to me. The racism became the primary characteristic of the writing, not a secondary one that could be understood and explained away in light of Conrad's cul-tural background and historical situation. And I understood that I shouldn't teach *The Heart of Darkness* unless I was ready to deal explicitly with the text's racism and condemn Conrad.

Last year, more than twenty years after this incident, I read an essay by the Nigerian novelist Chinua Achebe entitled "An Image of Africa: Racism in Conrad's *Heart of Darkness*" (in *Hopes and Impediments*, Doubleday, 1989, pp. 1-20) which con-firmed my analysis of the Conrad story. Achebe, after making his case against Conrad, states quite unambiguously, "The point of my observations should be quite clear by now, namely that

Joseph Conrad was a thoroughgoing racist. That this simple truth is glossed over in criticisms of his work is due to the fact that white racism against Africa is such a normal way of thinking that its manifestations go completely unremarked." (page 11)

I learned from Akmir's reading techniques how to unlearn habits of mine that let such racism in books pass unexamined. Before knowing him, I was not attuned to many of the nuances of racist implication because I was not the victim of racism. I did not suffer through every offensive phrase I encountered when reading, nor did I experience rage when racism was cloaked in the authority of tradition or the language of excellence. The lack of that sensitivity bothered me, and I had to unlearn this insensitivity to biased yet traditional ways of speaking and writing. In addition, I had to learn how to choose my own language and learn to make the avoidance of racist reference habit. I had to think very carefully about talking about "dark intents" and "black deeds"; to avoid using comparisons like "civilized/primitive," and "sophisticated/ unsophisticated"; and to eliminate characterizations like "disadvantaged" and "deprived." I had to learn to think from the perspective of someone who had not-learned racist language, and that experience has been an important part of my growth and development. Akmir's insistence upon the details of racist reference influenced how I read, speak, and write in much the same way that current feminist writing is influencing me. For me it was a matter of unlearning what could be called habits of inclusion and exclusion. Akmir's not-learning to speak or think in the racist ways of his teachers was, for him, a healthy response to racism. Unlearning racist and sexist language represents for me a similar commitment to struggle against racism and sexism in an everyday and thorough manner. It is not merely an intellectual exercise.

A few years ago in a college seminar I taught, one of the young women in the class took a stance towards not-learning sexist language that reminded me of Akmir's stance towards the language of racism. For example, she constantly corrected anyone in class who used masculine references to represent all people. She rephrased, out loud, statements such as "Man needs to do meaningful work" or "No matter what a doctor is doing he's always on call," and she would insist upon class time to rephrase every sentence in a story or article we read to make gender references exact. I agreed with her position but was initially annoyed at the time it was taking up in class. However, when some of the male students started baiting her for being so insistent on changing their habits of thought and ridiculing her as a "liberated girl," I supported her in her struggle and resolved to let the issue take over the class, if it came to that. I decided that, for those students, it was more important to deal with gender issues than the other educational issues we were supposed to be covering. I made gender and the power of language to mold thought the focus of the rest of the seminar. Unlearning the language of sexism with the guidance of someone who had not-learned it was a wonderful educational adventure for me and, I hope, for the rest of the students.

As a white male I am included in the male referent of most general phrases. I feel included in, though not necessarily described by, statements such as:

Man's actions are determined by egocentric motives.
Man is a rational animal.
All men are created equal.
It is man's fate to die.

Up to about ten or fifteen years ago it never occurred to me that women might not feel included in these statements. When this lack of inclusion was first pointed out to me, I put it down to historical circumstances of no current significance —nothing to take too seriously. The use of the male pronoun "he" in sentences such as "If a person wants something, he should fight for it" seemed comfortable and ordinary. I had developed a habit of inclusion that was comfortable to me because I was included. It wasn't comfortable to the excluded, to my wife or daughters, as my student pointed out to me. She was right. Exclusion, whether based on gender, race, class, or any other category, is a way of insulting and injuring people. I taught myself to unlearn the habits of what could be called male-talk by thinking of her as a reader when I read, until sensitivity to gender reference became habit.

Unlearning racist and sexist language habits has generalized, and I have learned new habits of inclusion and exclusion in reference. I think about nouns and pronouns and their references with greater precision than before, and I raise political questions about language in ways that has increased my insight into miseducation through language. For example, when I read "American teenagers think that," or "teachers believe that," or "the average American is," I have to stop and search for the specifics of the reference. Does the average American teenager live in Harlem or Hanover? Does the teacher work in a private school or a suburban school or a public school? Who has been honored to be the average American of the week? Claims like these, so common in the media and in school textbooks, dismiss complex issues with glib generalizations. Sloppy habits of reference lead not only to loose thinking but to the continued avoidance of dealing with social, racial, and gender issues that must be solved in order for this society to approximate its claims to democracy.

I had to unlearn to use the pronoun "he" to refer to all people. I can, however, imagine actively not-learning it just as Akmir not-learned racist language. Not-learning it would have consisted of being aware of the problem from the start, knowing as a child that adult habits of speech were biased and choosing to oppose these habits. I might have, for example, insisted on pointing out to my teacher that the title of our history book, *Man and His World*, was not merely imprecise but insulting. I could have then gone on to underline all of the incorrect references to the male and made a point of correcting the historical record. If I took the matter a step farther and insisted that the issues I raised be central to our discussion of history and called for a vote to change the name of the subject to herstory-and-history, or to theirstory, it's likely that the teacher would try to shut me up, the counselor would call me a learning and discipline problem, and the principal threaten to expel, transfer, or refer me, all of which happened to Akmir because of his racism not-learning project.

Not-learning and unlearning are both central techniques that support changes of consciousness and help people develop positive ways of thinking and speaking in opposition to dominant forms of oppression. Not-learning in particular requires a strong will and an ability to take the kinds of pressure exerted by people whose power you choose to question. Akmir and I often talked about the quality of his school experiences. He refused to drop out. He decided that he would sit right in the Wilderness of North America and openly not-learn what was offered to him rather than simply drop out and join a total community of other non-learners. That meant having a response to every mention and reference to race, reading and monitoring one's reading for even the slightest implications of racism, speaking very carefully and precisely, revising everything said in order to eliminate the white version of reality.

I once asked Akmir if he ever thought beyond his not-learning and the time it took up. He said that he did, that he wanted to use that not-learning to clear a space for himself to learn without feeling oppressed by words. He also wanted to write, to tell stories in a language that was positive and unselfconscious, that spoke of the life of black people without the need to qualify life by reference to white oppression. He said he wanted to write in a separated, separatist language, a post-revolutionary language. His dream was one of writing beyond race while affirming the quality of his experience and the history of his people.

His resistance to racism was the result of his vision of a world beyond racism, which he was afraid he would never see. It was this dream that propelled his not-learning. It was probably my respect for that dream and appreciation for what I learned through the creative efforts of his not-learning that made it possible for us to become as close as we did. It was 1967, and we talked about the meaning of the Vietnam War which he decided to resist. We also talked about how he could approach college in his clearing rather than through resistance. He wanted to learn, to become a writer and social activist, and he needed teachers who would teach beyond personal and institutional racism. Betty was one person who inspired him, and there were others who taught in the open enrollment program at City College. Akmir decided to move out of Harlem for a while. He felt his not-learning had to move him beyond the ghetto. Not-learning made him a discipline problem in school, but ironically it helped him to stay confident as a learner. It prevented him from thinking of himself as a failure or resigning himself to anything less than a fully developed life and self.

In late May of that year things began opening up for Akmir. He had gotten into the open enrollment program at City College, found a job at Teachers College, and moved into an apartment on the lower East Side. He began a series of stories about rebirth in what he called his "new language" and was planning a small volume of poetry. In June, however, he got his draft notice, on the same day he received a letter from City College informing him that he needed to show his high school diploma before he could be formally admitted. We visited his high school counselor, and I wrote up a course description and certificate of completion for the psychology course he had taken with Betty and me. The course was to serve as his citizenship class, his atonement for his not-learning in high school. The counselor, to our astonishment, refused to accept the class and told us that he wasn't sure Akmir was repentant enough. He informed us that he would release the diploma at his own pleasure. I pleaded and did everything I could to convince him to change his mind, including trying to use the prestige of Teachers College, where I was a research associate. There was no appeal, though, and we both left the school ready to blow the place up.

As it turned out Akmir didn't really need the diploma. City College had sent him the wrong letter. But he was devastated by that rejection, fearful of going to jail for being a war resister, and feeling, I believe, that the place he had spent his life clearing was violated or inaccessible. I never saw him alive again. That night, so far as I've been able to reconstruct, Akmir returned to his old neighborhood, ran into some friends, and ended up being abandoned in the emergency room of a nearby hospital where he died of an overdose of heroin—one more victim of what he spent his life not-learning.

Struggling to maintain integrity and hope may not always be the key to survival under conditions of oppression. Imitating your oppressors and trying to integrate yourself into their society might work better. Sometimes survival dictates swallowing one's pride and giving up self-respect. When there is no large scale movement for liberation, Akmir's alternatives, resistance and rebellion, are lonely and dangerous choices. Some of Akmir's friends became the violent, angry, and dangerous people white society imagined them to be. They succeeded on the streets for a while, but they also set themselves up for eventual self-destruction. Others did what their teachers and bosses told them to do and managed to integrate themselves into certain corners of the white world. Akmir was among those brave people who refused to abandon self-respect or allow himself to be consumed by hatred and self-hatred. Not-learning to think white was a strength that got him in trouble with his teachers, with some of the people he worked for, and with some of his own friends who, as much as they admired his integrity and resistance, felt he was too righteous, too uncompromising. He died pointlessly and in despair, but so far as I'm concerned his life was honorable and his death a tragic loss.

Over the years, I've come to believe that many of the young people who fail in our schools do so for the same reasons Akmir did and use many of the same strategies he adopted. I remember visiting some teacher friends in San Antonio, Texas, about fifteen years ago. I was there to help them eliminate anti-Latino racism in the public schools in the *barrios*, Latino ghettos. There were very few Latino teachers and no Latino administrators in *barrio* schools in the parts of San Antonio where my friends worked. Many of the administrators were Anglo, retired military personnel from the San Antonio air force base who had hostile, imperialist attitudes towards the children they taught and the communities they served. I was asked by a community group, as an outsider and as an Anglo myself, to visit a number of classrooms and participate in some work-shops discussing the specific ways in which racism functioned in their schools. In one junior high I was invited to observe a history class by a teacher who admitted that he needed help with this particular group of students, all of whom were Latino. The teacher gave me a copy of his textbook, and I sat in the back of the room and followed the lesson for the day which was entitled "The first people to settle Texas." The teacher asked for someone to volunteer to read and no one responded. Most of the students were slumped down in their desks and none of them looked directly at the teacher. Some gazed off into space, others exchanged glimpses and grimaces. The teacher didn't ask for attention but instead started to read the text himself. It went something like, "The first people to settle Texas arrived from New England and the South in . . ." Two boys in the back put their hands in their eyes, there were a few giggles and some murmuring. One hand shot up and that student blurted out, "What are we, animals or something?" The teacher's response was, "What does that have to do with the text?" Then he decided to abandon the lesson, introduced me as a visiting teacher who would substitute for the rest of the period, and left the room. I don't know if he planned to do that all along and set me up to fail with the students just as he did, or if his anger at being observed over-came him and he decided to dump the whole thing on me. Whatever the motivation, he left the room, and I was there with the students. I went up front, reread the sentence from the book, and asked the class to raise their hands if they believed what I had just read. A few of them became alert, though they looked at me suspiciously as I continued, "This is lies, nonsense. In fact, I think the textbook is racist and an insult to everyone in this room." The class woke up, and the same student who had addressed the teacher earlier turned to me and asked, "You mean that?" I said I did, and then he interrupted and said, "Well, there's more than that book that's racist around here."

A few of the other students nodded, and then the class went silent. It was up to me to continue with what I'd opened up or close the conversation down and protect the teacher. I decided to continue on, saying I didn't know their teacher but that I had run into more than one racist who was teaching and ought to be thrown out by the students and their parents. I added that it was obvious that the textbook was racist—the racism was there for everyone to read—but that I wondered how they detected racism in their teachers. The class launched into a serious and sophisticated discussion of the ways racism manifested itself in their everyday lives at school. And they described the stance they took in order to resist that racism and yet not be thrown out of school. It amounted to nothing less than full-blown, cooperative not-learning. They accepted the failing grades not-learning produced in exchange for the passive defense of their personal and cultural integrity. This was a class of school failures, and perhaps, I believed then and still believe, the repository for the positive leadership and intelligence of their generation.

Willed not-learning consists of a conscious and chosen refusal to assent to learn. It manifests itself most often in withdrawal or defiance and is not just a school-related phenomena. I recently discovered a version of a traditional religious and peace song which goes, "I ain't gonna learn war no more." Learning to make war is the opposite of learning to make peace. Many people who never learned to make war are told they must learn to make war when their nation decides to fight. During those times, pacifists and other people who choose non-violent ways have to not-learn to make war despite strong social pressures to do so. Poor people have to not-learn despair if they are to survive. Christians have to not-learn pride and arrogance. And on the opposite end of the moral spectrum, soldiers have to not-learn to care about the lives of the "enemy," and the boss has to not-learn to care about the sufferings of fired employees. Throughout life, there may be as much occasion for not-learning as there is occasion for learning. It is uncomfortable to talk about the need to reject certain kinds of learning and reassuring to look at learning in a positive way, but without studying not-learning we can get only a partial view of the complex decisions facing people as they choose values and decide upon actions. I am just beginning to understand the importance of not-learning in the lives of children, and I urge other people to think and write about roads people choose to not-travel and how those choices define character and influence destiny.

In rethinking my teaching experience in the light of not-learning, I realize that many youngsters who ask impertinent questions, listen to their teachers in order to contradict them, and do not take homework or tests seriously are practiced not-learners. The quieter not-learners sit sullenly in class, day-dreaming and shutting out the sound of their teacher's voice. They sometimes fall off their chairs or throw things across the room or resort to other strategies of disruption. Some push things so far that they get put in special classes or get thrown out of school. In all of these cases, the youngsters' minds are never engaged in learning what the teacher is trying to teach. On that level, no failure is possible since there has been no attempt to learn. It is common to consider such students dumb or psychologically disturbed. Conscious, willed refusal of schooling for political or cultural reasons is not acknowledged as an appropriate response to oppressive education. Since students have no way to legitimately criticize the schooling they are subjected to or the people they are required to learn from, resistance and rebellion is stigmatized. The system's problem becomes the victim's problem. However, not-learning is a healthy, though frequently dysfunctional, response to racism, sexism, and other forms of bias. In times of social movements for justice, such refusal is often turned to more positive mass protest and demonstration and to the development of alternative learning situations. For example, during the 1960s in New York, students who maintained their integrity and consciously refused the racist teachings of their segregated schools became leaders in school boycotts and teachers of reading and African American history in Freedom schools.

I've known such student leaders and have had the pleasure of working with some of them. Jamila L., the student-body president of an alternative high school I worked at during the late 1960s, told me that in the regular school she had spent four years in a special education class drinking orange juice, eating Graham Crackers, and pretending she couldn't read. The whole act was to keep from hitting several of her teachers who she knew were racist. In fact, she was an avid reader of romances and of Black history. She used special education to keep herself in school because her grandmother wanted her to graduate from high school. At our school she was a representative to the school board, helped develop projects and write proposals, and led students in a struggle against racist officers in the juvenile bureau of the local police department.

Jamila was not exceptional. There are many leaders and creators hidden away in the special classes of our schools, running wild in the halls, and hanging out in the bathrooms. In 1967, the poet June Jordan asked me to introduce her to some seniors from Benjamin Franklin High School which, at that time, was the only high school in Harlem. She was writing an article (published under the name June Meyer, "You Can't See the Trees for the School," *The Urban Review*, December 1967, Vol. 2 No. 3, New York, pp. 11-15) on what these students planned to do with their futures. Two of the students were at the bottom of their class and two had done well in school. Jordan described the first two this way:

> Paul Luciano and Victor Hernandez Cruz are friends. Neither of them thinks of graduation, next January, as anything except a time of "getting out" of the school, *per se*. Paul regards the expected "little piece of paper" (the diploma) a proof that you have been "whitey-fied" for four years.

In the course of their conversation Paul says:

> The (school's) program is a very confusing system. There's nobody to explain it to you. They just, you

know, like pat you on the back. People tell me if you don't go along with the program, you'll mess up your whole life.

I say then, well, to hell with my life. You have to take some kind of stand. Everything you learn is lies.

It's their education.   Not mine.
It's their history.   Not mine.
It's their language.   Not mine.
You name it. It's theirs.   Not mine.

A white teacher, he has not lived the life. He cannot relate any of the things to me. So I'm bored.

And Victor goes on a bit later:

George Washington had slaves, man. You know one time he traded a black man for a pig? . . . We told the librarian we wanted a picture of Malcolm X. We said we would supply our own picture and everything. But she said, "No." We wanted his picture up there with George Washington and Thomas Rickerson . . . the librarian said he preached hate. He! . . . We asked the librarian to get the *Autobiography of Malcolm X*. She said, "Some books you have to wait three years." It's still not there.

I wonder how many times this situation, so similar to the one portrayed over twenty years later in Spike Lee's movie *Do the Right Thing* where there is a conflict over putting up pictures of Malcolm X and Martin Luther King next to those of Italian American heroes in a neighborhood pizza parlor, has to be reenacted?

Later on in Jordan's article it turns out that both Victor and Paul were teaching reading at an education program sponsored by the Citizen's Council of Columbia University, a group that was involved in the student strike at Columbia that year. Both of them wanted to become teachers, the kind of teachers they imagined would empower students. And Victor, in one of his poems quoted in the article, expressed the feeling of most of the young people I have encountered who have chosen the route of not-learning:

> We would not be
> like flowers resting dead in some hill
> not even getting credit for its color
> or the way it smells.

In another poem written that year and published in his first volume of poetry entitled *Papo Got His Gun* (Calle Once Press, New York 1967, p. 6), Victor is much more explicit about the significance of not-learning. In talking about junior high school he writes:

> JHS was boss
> not because of what you taught me
> but because of what I learned
> which was not what you taught me

Until we learn to distinguish not-learning from failure and respect the truth behind this massive rejection of schooling by students from poor and oppressed communities, we will not be able to solve the major problems of education in the United States today. Risk-taking is at the heart of teaching well. That means that teachers will have to not-learn the ways of loyalty to the system and to speak out, as the traditional African American song goes, for the concept that everyone has a right to the tree of life. We must give up looking at resistant students as failures and instead turn a critical eye towards this wealthy society and the schools that it supports.

No amount of educational research, no development of techniques or materials, no special programs or compensatory services, no restructuring or retraining of teachers will make any fundamental difference until we concede that for many students the only sane alternative to not-learning is the acknowledgement and direct confrontation of oppression—social, sexual, and economic—both in school and in society. Education built on accepting that hard truth about our society can break through not-learning and can lead students and teachers together, not to the solution of problems but to direct intelligent engagement in the struggles that might lead to solutions.

Herbert Kohl has been both a teacher and a writer for over thirty years. He has taught in public schools in New York and California and has worked with teachers and students throughout the country. His education work and his writing have centered around making schools decent and democratic places of learning. Among his books are *36 Children*, *The Open Classroom*, *On Teaching*, and *Growing Minds*. He won the 1977 National Book Award for Children's Literature with Judith Kohl for their book, *View from the Oak*.

I Won't Learn from You! was typeset in 10 point Garamond Antiqua by Peregrine Publications and printed on acid-free Glatfelter Natural paper by Edwards Brothers Incorporated.